KNOW
I LOVED YOU
TODAY

poems by

Kenneth Francis Pearson

SCARMORA PRESS

Dedicated to the Memory of

Eddie Roth

September 5, 1996 to April 1, 2023

"... And when great souls die,
after a period, peace blooms,
slowly and always
irregularly. Spaces fill
with a kind of
soothing electric vibration.
Our senses, restored, never
to be the same, whisper to us.
They existed. They existed.
We can be. Be and be
better. For they existed."

- Maya Angelou

KNOW I LOVED YOU TODAY
Copyright © 2023 Kenneth Francis Pearson
All Rights Reserved

No part of this book may be reproduced in any form
or by any means without express written consent of
the author, excepting brief quotes used in reviews.

Send all inquiries to the following address:

Scarmora Press
17630 South Bronze Mountain Pass
Vail, AZ 85641

Scarmora Press is a subsidiary of
Pearson & Pearson, LLC.

First Edition
Printed in the United States of America
ISBN: 978-0-9768543-3-3

*This book is intended for entertainment purposes only.
Neither the author nor the publisher will assume any
responsibility for the use or misuse of any information
contained within this book.*

OTHER BOOKS BY
KENNETH FRANCIS PEARSON

The Old Leather Room
(Cyberwit, 2004)

Water Falls in Autumn: Verse vs. Adversity
(Amarcord Press, 2007)

Scattered
(Scarmora Press, 2021)

Catching Mist in the Wind
(Scarmora Press, 2022)

Table of Contents

Poems for Eddie	9
Winter	23
Autumn	29
Summer	37
Spring	47
The Life of Eddie Roth	57
Acknowledgements	59
Additional Information	61

Poems for Eddie

free from
the long nights
of suffering

                 - Ueda Gosengoku

Know I Loved You Today

If I don't make it 'til tomorrow,
know that I loved you today.

in all our tiny moments
of peace and solitude,
our eyes glancing, and
touching the infinite of the universe.

in our moments of laughter, and
sadness, and heartache, and triumph,
know you were always in my heart.

in our moments of thought,
when separated by distance,
memories forming a river of connection,
a pathway back to where you are,

I want nothing more,
than for you to know -

I
       loved
              you
                      today.

it is not fair to expect tears,
to bear the burden of long-ago memories,

to reflect every smile, every heartache,
every sleepless worry.

to capture the echoes
of laughter and sadness.

to pull from the sky, the moon,
and the sun, and encapsulate them
in a galaxy of our own existence.

yet, they are steadfast,
and continue to stream down my cheeks,
unannounced, and I still welcome them,

because they are my chance
to remember ... you.

he should've outlived the oak, or
grown larger than the redwood,

but sometimes saplings suffocate in winter,
beneath the weight of mounting snow.

resilient is the tree, and
as her life matures,
and branches extend,
and roots take hold,

and as she breathes the air,
and greets the sky,
and the sun,
and the moon,

as she survives storms,
and droughts,
and hostility,
and indifference,

there are times when a branch
will splinter, and split itself in two,
crashing to the earth,
beneath the weight of gravity,

and remains the scar for all to see,
the broken limb, covered by time,
the constancy of loss, sensed in its blemish,
and the memories of its presence.

and until she begins to fade,
and her leaves wither, and her roots fail,
and the earth finally reclaims her,
the scar will always remain.

it feels as if, every so often,
the world should stop and
acknowledge the kindness
that exists.

and perhaps it does,
and perhaps it did for you,

but it moved forward,
indifferent, like it always seems to do,
while ripples of your death were shared,
in the crashing waves of the infinite.

and it feels like nothing has changed,
and nothing ever will, even as
the arms of the universe have embraced you,
while grieving for the world's loss.

and I await the day, she
frees you – and scatters you
across the vastness of the universe,
as I close my eyes, open my heart,
and feel your energy pass through –

yes, I await the day.

I want to believe,
you were not alone,
that we were there with you,
in thoughts and memories,
as you closed your eyes,
and took one final breath,
before embarking on the infinite journey,
across the universe.

I want to believe,
you were not afraid,
that we were there to comfort you,
in mind and spirit,
as you were there for all of us, and,
as you stared at the unknown,
you could see the greatness of your life.

I want to believe,
that in your final moments,
you were comforted by the love
of a world who loved you so dearly,
a world who could see your being with clarity,
even if your search for sunlight
was sometimes shaded by clouds.

This ...

                              ... I want to believe ...

it's time I spend now,
reliving our memories,
that I am at peace.

he was once the moon,
cycles shrouded in darkness –
now, he is the sun.

winter came early,
the season's blanket of snow,
covered in ashes.

so many words
left unsaid – now you rest,
amongst the stars.

sometimes the sun
can be the difference …
sometimes the moon.

the full moon proudly
takes its place among the stars –
a tearful goodbye.

his energy
spread across the universe –
sips of black coffee.

most nights I cry,
at thoughts of your brevity
among the infinite.

I forget,
keys on the counter – and
your last words to me.

aimless we wander ...
until the coldness of night,
icy hand of death.

early spring sunrise,
the smell of honeysuckle
before last snowfall.

in early spring
earth covered in your ashes,
sun distanced by clouds.

even birds annoy,
after the ceremony –
ashes dissipate.

hours scrolling
through pictures, fear
of forgetting.

every day, moments

Winter

The woods are lovely, dark and deep,
But I have promises to keep,
And miles to go before I sleep,
And miles to go before I sleep.

- Robert Frost

remember the dead,
the souls of our ancestors –
distant mourning bells.

the telling of time,
rests in wrinkles of your hands'
creviced memories.

ice and snow sublime,
vapor hides lonely footprints –
glance from snow leopard.

blinded by sunlight –
pine needles pierce the shadows
of those left behind.

the ghosts of letchworth
haunt dilapidated halls –
numbers on headstones.

february sky,
hue of pink and blue –
a full morning moon.

the smell of orchids,
the only thing remembered,
at his funeral.

blanket of snow,
reverent branches bow –
trail of paw prints.

stars illuminate,
over western horizon –
february moon.

commute from work,
pink glaze from western sunset –
winter on red rock.

too tired ...
to stare at a sunset,
a chore.

winter wind on face ...
sun setting behind
bare tree branches.

Autumn

Where are the songs of Spring?
Ay, where are they?
Think not of them,
thou hast thy music too.

- John Keats

in blindness of night,
soft voice whispers ancient love –
selene peaks through clouds.

waterfall teardrops
outstretched arms embrace sorrow –
blinding basin mist.

time drifts away –
the sun disappears
behind the day moon.

footprints on pavement
time whispers in rustling leaves –
sun walks down mountain.

leaves flutter,
a reverent bend of branches –
grey clouds split the sky.

a reflective mind
wanders into peacefulness –
driftwood on the shore.

happiness eludes
during parade of joy – a
melancholy heart.

still night,
lightning splits sky –
crickets chirp.

clouds drift ...
over orange horizon,
mars over moon.

teardrop stain
on handwritten letter –
plane on the runway.

sun touches
the constant of the earth –
time moves with shadows.

beauty rests
in sunsets – another day
forever gone.

silhouette of trees
illuminated,
by sunset backdrop.

insects scurrying
in gleam of a sunset sky –
calm rock of the chair.

Summer

As imperceptibly as Grief
The Summer lapsed away—
Too imperceptible at last,
To seem like Perfidy.

                 - Emily Dickinson

flowers in her hair,
draped bouquet in golden locks –
wisps the salty sea.

loneliness exists
in a barren desert sand
touched by the soft breeze.

it's the sun, she says,
our universe as it burns –
yet, we're still nothing.

tell them the story,
wolves in the dark night
and death, she says.

in the dull lamplight ...
a silhouette living the life,
of one thousand souls.

book read under lamp ...
as the words come to life,
so too does the world.

fresh cut grass –
in the closet
my father's baseball mitt.

in the neighborhood,
children playing a game of tag –
western clouds gliding.

she was tiny once,
then journeys around the sun –
yearly moon cycle.

as ants march,
so too
does the storm.

unified system ...
ants marching
on dirt hill.

breeze across pond,
ripple beneath lily pad –
mosquito's first bite.

lavender
draped over trellis –
the spider web.

closed eyes
warmth of the sun – setting
on the horizon.

at sunset,
eye lashes catch gold –
prism dances.

stars appear
one by one –
streak of clouds.

stillness of the air
before the blink of my eyes –
peregrine in flight.

calmness of wind,
in moments before sunrise –
coyote in brush.

on walkway ...
petals glide to the rhythm
of ants.

Spring

And 'tis my faith that every flower
Enjoys the air it breathes.

- William Wordsworth

in the grass, a fawn ...
nose burrowed into frail legs,
raindrops in puddles.

mid-spring day,
cold morning, warm afternoon –
jacket on park bench.

sunlight crests the east,
touching the tips of mountains,
a distant dog barks.

a clink of glasses,
the air filled with promises,
comfort in your lips.

with bare, outstretched arms
she basks in apricity –
love awaits nightfall.

deep pastel blanket
covers the cool dry desert –
a sunset goodnight.

rain upon my brow
petrichor and rainbows –
a daydream dance.

cool petrichor wind,
gentle tuesday afternoon –
she touches my hand.

a flowered sundress
in the spring wind dances
a dandelion.

coyote howl –
in the dawn of morning,
at the bus stop.

rabbit crawls
under broken gate,
to spring garden.

he touches the world,
and in the palm of his hand –
a budding seed.

the journey begins,
with a gentle push from wind –
the seed to sapling.

as roots sprout from seed,
and earth covers the sunlight –
lovers touching hands.

in garden,
clearing bladder,
clearing mind.

early spring ...
koi swimming gayly
on water's surface.

old pinecone,
shares wind and branch
with budding new.

cocoon hangs
from blossoming flower,
soon the butterfly.

first song
from the morning bird –
sun greets sky.

beat of taiko drum
feet upon the rocks –
paper flowers.

first of april ...
warm sun touches face
I lay in grass.

the moon follows me,
as I walk the foothill path –
dew drips from flowers.

mist coats the mountain,
morning sun across the valley –
the shadows of trees.

This book is dedicated in loving memory of my nephew, Edward "Eddie" Roth.

Eddie's curiosity led him on adventures across the globe and down uncharted paths. He embraced every new experience with joy and shared that enthusiasm freely. Eddie poured his full spirit into everything he did, whether mastering the drums or starting a new business venture. He lived life to the fullest.

Above all, Eddie loved and cherished his family. He was always ready with a laugh, a hug, or heartfelt words of advice. Losing him leaves an immense hole in all our hearts.

While we all deeply mourn his passing, portions of this book are meant to commemorate Eddie's extraordinary life and indomitable spirit. May his memory be a blessing and comfort to his family and many friends. And may his unbridled passion for living continue to inspire us all.

To read more about the life of Eddie, please visit:

https://betzlerlifestory.com/obituaries/
eddie-roth.143142

Acknowledgements

Awarded Outstanding at the
2022 Arizona Matsuri Festival

deep pastel blanket
covers the cool dry desert –
a sunset goodnight.

First appeared in the anthology "To Live Here"
by The Wee Sparrow Press

the smell of orchids,
the only thing remembered,
at his funeral.

First appeared on The Wee Sparrow Press
Instagram Page

in blindness of night,
soft voice whispers ancient love –
selene peaks through clouds.

FOR MORE INFORMATION

www.kfpearson.com
www.scarmorapress.com
Instagram - @kennethfrancispearson
TikTok - @kfppoetry

www.ingramcontent.com/pod-product-compliance
Lightning Source LLC
Chambersburg PA
CBHW062104290426
44110CB00022B/2715